Personal

BRAND

and

CV

The essential guide to differentiating yourself in the job market - so you stand out from all the others chasing the same position

BERNARD PEARCE
The Executive Career Transition Specialist

Published in the United Kingdom by:
Career Inspirations

Cover design & layout by Velin@Perseus-Design.com

ISBN Number: 978-1-9996493-0-2 (Paperback)
978-1-9996493-1-9 (E-book)

Contents

For Executives and Senior Managers - this book is for you.

It delivers unprecedented insight to transform how you:

- Recognise and articulate how good you really are.

- Understand why you are worth the salary you seek.

- Present yourself more effectively and professionally.

- Can be better presented than competitors for the same job.

- Will improve your chances in the job market, at your level.

- Can breakthrough corporate glass doors and ceilings.

- Can become who you are capable of being.

Introduction

The job market is tough – and for the Executive and Senior Manager, the higher up the organisational pyramid they go, the tougher it gets.

Good career transition advice and support for Executives and Senior Managers is sadly lacking. Even with the wealth of self-help guidelines on the market, there is little aimed specifically at you – meaning that you might approach the job market in the same way you did either on leaving university or when your career was at a much earlier and less developed stage.

So it is time we corrected that situation and I'm sharing over 25 years of experience, where I have developed and used unique approaches to help countless hundreds of people like you make the step change you need.

Most Executives and Senior Managers facing job change, whether by their own choice or forced upon them by circumstances outside their control, don't appreciate, or can't articulate, just how good they are. They are often held back from recognising how good they can be, or even from appreciating their potential value to another organisation.

Your Personal Brand and CV must therefore present you as someone special – not just 'one more highly-paid person looking for another job'.

Those at senior levels, often find the process of replacing their income source quite challenging – where their self-esteem, self-confidence and self-worth are tested to the extreme – an experience that often leads to them lowering their sights to match their lower sense of self – which is not the best state of mind in which to be looking to replace an income, or to secure a much better job!

Many might have previously been quite settled in a 'comfort rut' in either the wrong job, or the wrong organisational culture, where they probably performed well, but now find their role is no longer needed, or their work has been absorbed into other roles for which they are not the right fit.

Often too, that 'comfortable' environment might have prevented them becoming the truly successful person they are capable of being!

So you, the Executive or Senior Manager facing career transition, either through your own volition or circumstances outside your control, this book – the first of three that collectively span the entire job hunting process - is essential reading.

It will enable you to:

- Articulate your value to another organisation!
- Present yourself as someone of real value!
- Enable potential employers to understand your value to them!

The world needs highly skilled people to lead companies well; but those highly skilled people also need to understand and articulate their value too!

If you 'don't know' how good you are, how can you expect others to know?

Hoping that someone else will be able to work out your value, because you're not able or willing to do so, is about as useless as sitting watching the TV and expecting a job to come knocking on your door!

The job market is tough, but organisations always need really good people who bring that something special – someone like you!.

This is your first step towards your future - I'm already cheering you on to succeed!

The impact of technological innovation

The last 100 years have seen the most dramatic changes that human beings have ever had to adjust to – and that rate of change is increasing thanks to technological innovation.

In 1939 – it was considered that TV would never be a substitute for radio because you had to keep looking at it!

In 1943 – the chairman of IBM considered that there was only a worldwide market for just five computers!

In 1950 – the computing power in the whole world was less than that contained in a musical greeting card today!

In 1980 – a single chip contained 6000 tiny transistors and by 2016 it was over 7.2 billion!

In 1993 – there were just 14m internet users, but by 2020 there will be over 50 billion devices connected!

In 1995 – most homes didn't have a computer and only a few had a telephone not connected by a cable to its base!

Now – most homes are connected to the Internet; most people have a phone, tablet or laptop that connects to the World Wide Web which is fast transitioning into the Mobile Media Mode. We now have cloud computing, artificial intelligence and driverless cars – all of which demand jobs that never existed before!

Children now see this as the norm; what awaits them in their future?

1.

The Future of Work

"The fourth industrial revolution is creating prospects of a future that few fully comprehend, but the implications for the world of work are already taking shape". "Society has survived three such upheavals before, and has emerged stronger and better each time".

(Raconteur – Independent Publisher – 2017)

For those who are entering the job market for the first time, seeking to improve their position in it, or indeed merely even trying to survive in it, it is essential to be aware of what is happening and to be ready to adapt to the situation, adopt new ways of working and to be at the leading, not the trailing edge of change.

We have all seen those who have struggled to keep their head above the swirling waters of change, trying to retain an earning level whilst being discarded by those who no longer want what they were. Organisations need those who embrace change and bring the techniques and thinking levels that are essential for future growth and survival.

A survey by PwC (PricewaterhouseCoopers) of 10,000 global consumers seeing what will change the way people work over the next 5 to 10 years, identified technology breakthroughs, resource scarcity and climate change, shifts in global economic power, and demographic shifts, as being the major influencers.

Workforce trends, identified by ADP, a US management and software services company, indicated a major shift in the use of technology, employees being able to define their own work schedule and work from mobile devices. In addition, a shift in hierarchical and departmental structure and employees pay based upon their personal contribution, will transform the reliance on traditional working relationships.

Transformation, however, disrupts the norm and is never a smooth process, particularly when so many elements are all combining to create what might be seen as the ultimate business storm to create the massive shift into the fourth industrial revolution – but this time on a truly global scale, with all nations seeking to be leading players in it, in some way.

The pace of change, eagerly gathering momentum in this modern age, demands that skill shortages will need to be addressed quickly, shifts in educational preparation must be slicker and those already in work must learn to adapt to the demands of a new workplace or risk drowning in the flotsam with those who are unaware, or too slow to adapt.

Organisations seeking to secure their place within this turmoil will be pursuing the hunt for the best talent, the most skilled, the brightest minds; those with new product innovation, ideas and solutions, and with the drive, attitude and commitment to make things happen.

Technology will help break the geographical, cultural and language barriers, but it will be essential that the right people are engaged to work together, contribute their own personal strengths, and become a valued constituent part of their organisation's overall objectives, whether on a full-time employee basis, or as a key contributor to a specific activity.

Change will inevitably drive some jobs out of existence, but it is too late to apply an overly defensive, Government-blaming, head-in-the-sand, Luddite approach. Change is already happening, and it will continue to happen and force some out of their familiar comfort-ruts, to find new roles with different demands.

This modern workplace is not just for the 'young thrusters'. It needs those with 'old experience' too. It will span generations, where old skills combine with new technology, new ideas combine with trusted processes, and diversity brings the best people together and brings the best out of people.

At the same time, moves away from traditional nine-to-five working hours, departmental structure, formalised process and controls; and employer-employee relationships, heralds an increase in looser project-led associations, home-working, portfolio careers, self-employment and more collaboratively networked working teams.

In 1986 it was forecast that 65% of those working, by the year 2006, would be doing jobs that didn't even exist in 1986. The pace of change is gathering speed and it is recognised that 65% of graduates in 2018, will be doing jobs in the next five years that don't currently exist!

The Times Newspaper reported in July 2017 on the changing world of work, with some young people already doing jobs that didn't exist when they were still at school, including:

- **Brexit Planner** – those operating either in Government departments involved with overall negotiations; or in a wide range of commercial global organisations planning their operations within the shifting sands of uncertainty.

- **Drone Photographer** – aerial-imaging specialists providing functional or creative images for a growing range of needs including: hotels, golf courses, construction or insurance companies; and of course film and television!

- **Gaming Shoutcaster** – commentators at major gaming or e-Sport events who ensure that the often fast and frantic action being played and displayed on a screen is understandable to those watching in an arena or at home.

- **Data Robotics Engineer** – designers of new automation and artificial intelligence solutions that will increase productivity and the efficiency of business processes, some of which can be carried out efficiently by robots.

As the dynamic job market evolves, it is also important to recognise the potential 'disconnect' between the world of education and business reality; between subject specialisms and work interests; and that businesses often don't see their responsibility being the training of graduates and others in basic work-related skills.

It is essential, therefore, that every individual accepts personal responsibility for their on-going development; for articulating their potential value to current or prospective employers more clearly, effectively and confidently; and so to protect their own employability - not leaving decisions on their value solely in the hands of others.

So, as organisations seek to adapt to the increasing demands of global change and competition, survival will force them to adopt new technologies, react quickly to new opportunities; and introduce new working structures and practices.

This will, without question, have a huge emotional impact on their workforce as they in turn are expected to quickly learn new skills, perform new tasks and respond positively to the new demands made of them.

The future world of work will be tough for everyone, but even tougher for those at senior levels. Resistance is futile.

Executives and senior managers must, therefore, be ready to either step-up to meet these challenges, or be prepared to find alternative employment options.

In either case, they will need to clearly understand and articulate who they are, where they add real value, how they adapt to change and bring others through it; and how they will inject new energy and enthusiasm to drive progress.

Those who do not have a Personal Brand and a CV that clearly presents their real value, either internally or to new prospective employers might be in danger of losing out, or find themselves on the wrong side of future decision-making.

The future belongs to those who embrace it, drive it and enjoy the journey; more importantly, it is there for those prepared for it.

EMOTIONAL CHANGE MODEL

Where change is instigated by a third party

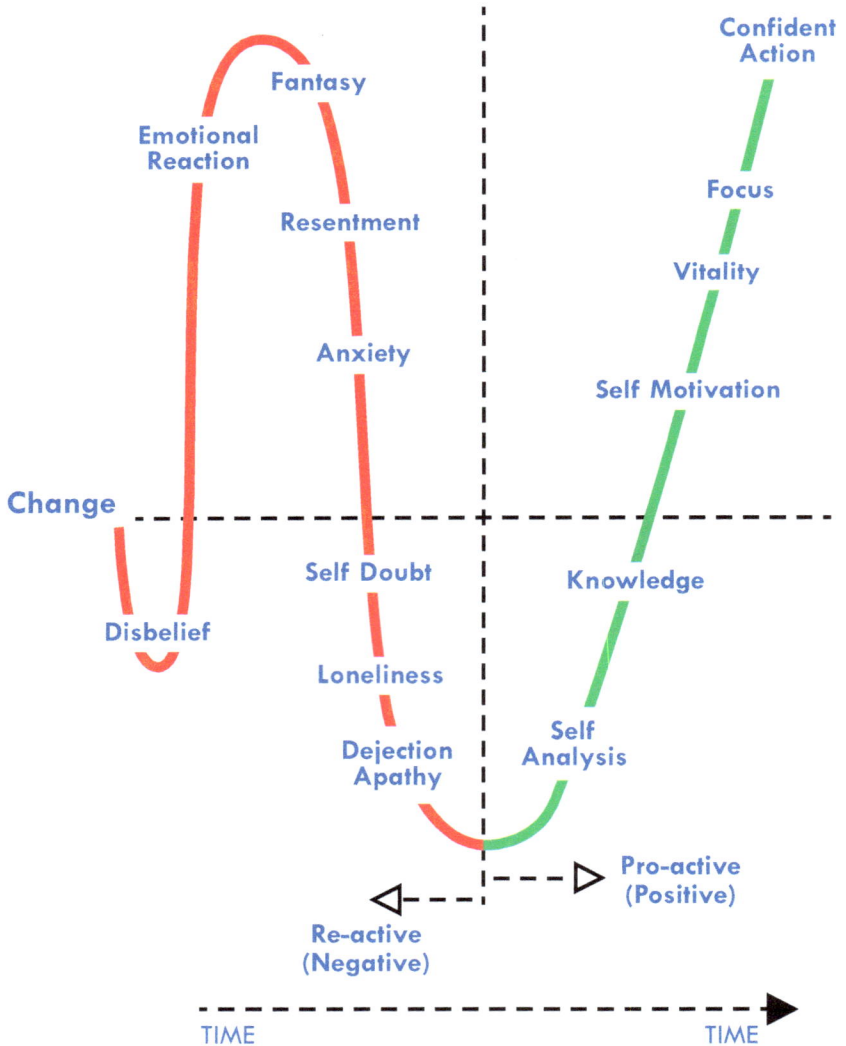

Fantasy

Emotional
Reaction

Resentment

Anxiety

Confident
Action

Focus

Vitality

Self Motivation

Change

Self Doubt

Disbelief

Loneliness

Dejection
Apathy

Knowledge

Self
Analysis

Pro-active
(Positive)

Re-active
(Negative)

TIME

TIME

After Hopson and Scally

2.

The Emotional Effects of Change

W e all experience change in our personal or working lives.

Change can be positive, exciting and energising when it's your idea or is meeting your objectives, but it has a totally different effect when it is not your own idea – when the decision is taken away from you and you have little control or influence over how it will affect you personally.

You, like many of the people reading this, might be experiencing a shift in circumstances that are not of your own choosing. As such, there is a huge risk of reacting like a rabbit in headlights and not doing anything – not knowing where to start, or worse, knee-jerking into fight or flight mode whilst your emotions are not under control.

Our automatic response to enforced change is often a combination of disbelief and resistance, as our survival instinct kicks in to protect us against perceived threats, or from what we don't fully understand.

Without fully appreciating the implications, or likely outcomes of proposed changes, our natural response is most probably going to be negative. In addition we tend to grieve the loss of what we had, until we start to think more positively about the possibilities and opportunities the enforced change might have for us.

This section will help you move towards a more positive position and help get you back in control of your own situation and future.

Emotions fluctuate of course and don't follow a linear one-directional process. The Emotional Change Model is not a road map. It shows the range of emotions you might experience, but the information here will help to keep you on track and take a more proactive approach to securing the future you aspire to.

The Reactive – Red-Light Emotions

Disbelief
At the point of finding out that circumstances are about to change our situation, we sometimes find it hard to take the message in. We say things like 'I can't believe it', whether the news is about a huge lottery win or the loss of a job. The important thing to recognise is that this reaction is normal – it doesn't signify the end of the world, even if it might feel like it!

Emotional Reaction

Our normal reaction to an announcement of enforced change – that which you have no control or influence over – can manifest itself as somewhere between anger or fear, as our natural sense of self-preservation takes over. This is also a natural response phase - it starts to help shake us out of denial and mentally start the process of understanding the situation - even if we still don't like the effect it might have on us! We can then start to move forward.

Fantasy

Whilst caught in this sense of self-preservation, many start to seek the opportunity that it might present – the 'what might be in it for me' syndrome that might even create unrealistic expectations, or even release a previously supressed ambition, but our emotional state can often get us thinking in non-rational ways.

Resentment

A lack of control or influence over the circumstances that are now affecting us, sometimes draws out some additional or associated factors – many of which might have lain buried or dormant for years. Negative feelings might become evident, particularly if we feel either unrewarded or unrecognised for work done, assistance given, or where others have received accolades for effort we have made.

Anxiety

Enforced change naturally creates anxiety. We all have mouths to feed and bills to pay, and the possibility of not being able to do either often throws us into a panic – with the possible danger that we start applying for jobs we can't do, don't want to do, or that will force us to work in environments we don't like and locations too far away from home. This knee-jerk reaction is rarely beneficial.

Self-Doubt

Enforced change is renowned for developing negative emotions and creating vivid images of the challenges we face. Being over or under qualified, too young or too old, too experienced or not, told you were over paid in a previous role, believing that there are no opportunities or vacancies you can apply for, ultimately creating a feeling that you might never be able to get a good job. Whilst understood, for those who seek professional support, these feelings are proved unfounded.

Loneliness

The thought of leaving the people we work with often creates a feeling of isolation – no longer being part of the former team. It is important to recognise, however, that those people might also be a huge help to you in finding a new job, so it's important to stay in touch with them – they will appreciate an opportunity to help, so let them in!

Dejection and Apathy

All these negative connotations associated with enforced change can, for those who allow themselves to be overwhelmed by them, drive down our emotional reserves and make the way forward feel a huge burden with little hope – so why bother? The reality is that, those who secure professional help and support through this difficult time tend to come out the other side, far happier, wiser and with a good next job!

The Proactive – Green-Light Emotions

Self-Analysis

Sitting in front of your PC and brain-dumping information into a CV template, whilst hoping that the reader might be able to make sense of what you can't be bothered to do correctly, doesn't make sense.

Most people either creating or updating their CV, do so without undertaking a full review of who they are, what they really want to do, what they are really good at doing, and what evidence they could provide to demonstrate it all.

Self-analysis is a positive exercise and is an important part of rebuilding confidence, self-esteem and boosts our emotional reserves.

Knowledge

The personal benefit of rebuilding self-worth, by drawing positive information together that clearly demonstrates your value to a prospective employer, cannot be under-estimated. Chapters 4, 5, 6 and 7 demonstrate a very straightforward way of doing this.

These guidelines, when followed carefully, will simplify the process and enable the creation of a very powerful CV that will present you at your best, for the role you aspire to - see the Chapter 8 on CV writing.

Self-Motivation

You will soon appreciate the hugely beneficial effect on your emotional well-being, of fully recognising and being able to articulate what you have done, the difference you've made, and the potential you can bring to a prospective employer. This information, formally presented in a dynamic and robust CV, in a way that clearly articulates your value to a potential employer, will further boost your self-esteem and self-motivation. Imagine, then, your level of confidence when discussing this at interview.

Vitality – Energy

The experience of enforced job change can be quite emotionally draining and you might not really appreciate the exhausting and energy-sapping process you are going through. Disappointment and delay will affect your emotional well-being and that of your immediate family.

Having a powerful CV – and being able to demonstrate your value to your immediate family as well as those you meet in the process of job-searching can restore your personal confidence and re-charge your emotional reserves. When you and those around you feel better and stronger, you will perform better in your job search and at interview too!

Focus

When you are able to present yourself positively, when you have your energy levels back on track and are now able to perform at your best and high-performing standards, it is important that you maintain your morale and motivation by doing the right things, in the right way.

Maintaining a focus on your key objective - the right job, in the right sort of organisation and in the right geographical location, will ensure you avoid the energy-sapping job search processes most people follow.

Confident Action

Your energy reserves might still be fragile as you handle the emotional peaks and troughs of job-searching. Maintaining them at a high level is key to ensuring you follow a constructive approach. Following positive guidance will avoid you falling into the bad habits of those who have neither learned how to conduct a positive job search, nor enjoyed professional support and guidance to avoid bad job-searching habits.

Beware then, the self-appointed 'expert' who knows nothing, but might negatively influence your outcome.

If you don't define yourself, others will do it for you – and you may not like or agree with their description!

Personal branding is the practice of people marketing themselves and their careers as brands. While previous self-help management techniques were about self-improvement, the personal-branding concept suggests instead that success comes from self-packaging.

Wikipedia

"A brand is a relationship, not a statement. And a strong brand is a special relationship, fuelled by a strong belief system and tied to the principle of giving exceptional value."
David McNally & Karl D Speak – Be Your Own Brand

Personal brands should be important to everyone. Personal brands are not only for the entrepreneur that owns their own business. It is the secret sauce that can make you stand out from within a stack of resumes.

If you don't develop your own personal brand others will do it for you. Developing your personal brand is the proactive way of controlling your career development and how you are perceived in the marketplace.

A strong personal brand will impact your ability to get the right jobs, promotions, and increase your ability to attract talent and capital

Laura Luke – Marketing

3.

Your Personal Brand

Organisations increasingly seek to recruit specialists, not generalists, to fulfil their needs; and it is really important that individuals also recognise that specialists, not generalists, are held in higher regard and receive the better rewards for their efforts.

Those seeking to survive in the future world of work, where little remains constant, will face an increasing demand for presenting themselves as high quality, high value, potential employees or even potential short-term or project-related assets. It is their responsibility to do so, not the responsibility of potential organisations to try and work it out for them!

We have all grown up with organisational and product Brands, where each is attempting to differentiate themselves from their key competitors - to appear more appealing, higher-performing or better value.

Your Personal Brand means clearly and consistently presenting who you are genuinely – your real value-adding strengths, combined with your personality, character, attitudes, and motivations; and being able to articulate them concisely and with confidence.

It is the real you – and you need to understand who you are, what you do, where you add value – and why others might want to employ you – every time they see you, whether that's through your CV, Social Media and right through to Interview and into that new job.

Most people approach the job market by trying to be someone, or worse, anyone that the employer might want, and in doing so unconsciously compromise just about everything that is important to them.

This often happens so much that they end up in the wrong job, doing the wrong things, for the wrong organisation and even in the wrong location.

This 'child-like' approach to a 'parent' organisation would be unheard of if you applied it to other major decisions in life.

When we approach life as a customer, spending our hard-earned savings, we would never allow others to dictate what we do.

How would we respond to:

- An Estate Agent who told us where we were going to live?
- A Car Salesperson who told us what car we will buy?
- A Travel Agent who told us where we were going on vacation?

When we are spending our money, on the new home that suits our needs, a car we will enjoy driving, or what might be our only real holiday of the year, it would be a complete waste of money if we weren't going to like it! Price tells us whether we can afford it, not whether it is right for us!

As a customer, we tend to have a much better idea of what our needs are, what budget we are working to, and how these things dovetail into our social and moral values.

If we are to transform our approach to career transition from 'child' to 'customer', we need to have a much clearer understanding of who we are, what it is we want, what things we like to do, what industry or sector we would like to work in, the level of seniority or sphere of influence we desire, and perhaps even more importantly for some, the geographical location or desired optimum commuting time.

And yet, all too often, people believe that this thinking is wrong - the 'old ways' are right - that they have to get what they can, where they can, and for what others see as their worth.

Well they are wrong.

If you have a clear understanding of your key value-adding strengths, your personality, working style, values and aspirations, then you can truly present yourself well as the authentic and exceptional person you are. After that, it's just a matter of finding those who need you, not those who need you to be someone you're not, but might attempt to be!

Chapter 4 continues with some key questions that need to be addressed carefully. They demonstrate a simple and straightforward approach, but many see the process as unnecessary and seek to circumnavigate it.

They are wrong, there is no easy way round it – so follow these simple guidelines, complete the simple exercises and the results will transform the way you understand what your Personal Brand is and how you later present it to others!

My desire is that you are spared the bruising nature of career change, by maintaining your authenticity right through the entire job search and interview process.

At interview and when job searching, you will need to be able to give brief, upbeat responses to typical questions. Being concise will prevent you getting bogged down in potentially difficult detail. Being upbeat will focus the listener on the positive – and interviewers, in particular are far too good at remembering the negatives.

It is absolutely vital therefore that you have prepared and rehearsed clear and consistent responses to the typical questions you will be asked hundreds of times.

Most people think that they both know themselves and can present themselves well. Well they don't. My 25 years of taking people through career transition, whether by their own decision, or enforced by others, consistently illustrates just how poorly people present themselves.

Most interviewers acknowledge disappointment in most interviewees – they were looking for someone different or better than the person presented at interview.

Following the guidelines in this book will prevent them saying something similar about you!

4.
Presentation Statements

The following subjects/questions will be discussed or asked hundreds of times as you meet contacts and recruiters through your job search journey. You must be able to answer them clearly, concisely and consistently – and remember that other people can only know what you tell them. You cannot expect them to fill in the gaps, try to see you in a better light than you present, or try work out things for themselves.

1. **YOUR LEAVING STORY:**
    (Why have you left or are looking to leave xxx Company?)

    Within 20 to 30 seconds, explain the circumstances that led to your present situation. This should be factual and non-emotional. It is more important to explain the driving forces behind the decision and the process that followed, rather than the terms you might be leaving on.

    It is better that you avoid talking about personality clashes, being badly treated, organisational incompetence, or lack of recognition or reward, as these may be received as 'bad-mouthing' your employer and prospective companies might fear you would talk about them in the same way. Additionally, you need to ensure that you are not perceived as someone carrying volumes of emotional baggage.

An example might be:

The company has gone through a major restructuring exercise and my role has been absorbed into other divisions. We have looked at alternative roles but there are none that would be challenging enough to keep me interested. So, rather than get trapped in the wrong role, I thought it was better to leave and find another role elsewhere. I have therefore agreed an exit strategy that will help them through the transition before I move on.

2.   YOUR JOB SEARCH STORY
(What are you looking to do now?)

Again, within 20 to 30 seconds, describe the perfect next job you aspire to – its job title, the level it would be at or your sphere of influence – local, national, Europe, EMEA, global? Additionally, it's important to state your preference on the type of organisation, the operating sector and your preferred geographical location. (Keeping your options open just indicates lack of clarity - and if you're not clear, how can anyone else help?)

Many hesitate with this in the expectation that they need to keep their options open, rather than closed, in the belief that a perfect role may appear in a different sector, or location.

Of course, it doesn't stop you looking elsewhere, but if the perfect opportunity came up and neither you nor anyone else knew that it was perfect, why would they bother telling you about it?

The reality is that, when people dare to create the specification for their perfect next job, the Universe tends to conspire to deliver!

Do either of these job search stories sound 'limiting'?

My perfect next role would be the Managing Director of a £50m to £100m turnover company in the electronics industry, with its HQ in Dublin and a global manufacturing and customer base. I would be particularly interested in one with an equity stake, or where the current ownership was looking to exit the business in a few years.

What I'm looking to build is a portfolio of activities including non-exec directorships in medium-sized manufacturing organisations with an international footprint; and consultancy roles, helping management teams address some of their complex business improvement challenges.

3. YOUR WORKING STYLE
(What are you like at work?)

A brief, one minute, summary of what you are like at work. It's about you as a person, not your job. It's the way you work; your personal values; what inspires or motivates you; and how you relate to, or interact with others.

Many people find this quite challenging, mostly because modesty gets in the way, they don't like blowing their own trumpet, or they can't think of anything good to say about themselves!

In either case, it's worth putting yourself in the position of others – those more senior than you who know you, those within your own peer group, and those who you have led or managed. Then ask what you think they might say if asked to say what you are like at work. Don't worry, you can edit out things you might not like!

4.   **YOUR CAREER OVERVIEW**
      (Take me through your career to date.)

A 3 to 4 minute overview, creating an interesting and engaging story of how you came to be where you are. This is your sales story, so weave in some key achievements that show how good you are!!

Start by reminding them of your current or last job, company and location, but no details - it's the wrong time - save them for the end!

Then go right back to the beginning, from graduation, and walk the reader/listener through your career, so that they appreciate the journey you've made and what you've achieved on the way. Give the year of each change point, and its reason – promotion etc - then end with the detailed information on your current/last role.

Ensure you include key aspects of your experience within your story that are particularly relevant to the role you are seeking.

5. **YOUR KEY VALUE-ADDING STRENGTHS**
   (Where do you add particular value?)
   (Developed further in Chapter 6)

   If you don't know where you add real value to an organisation, how can you expect potential employers to know? Often, we think that others will be able to work it out for themselves, if they take the trouble to find out; but how can they ever know more about you than you know about yourself?

   You cannot risk allowing other people to decide what you are good at, as they don't really know you, they have not done what you've done; and if you expect allow them to form their own opinion, they might not reach the right conclusion!

   It is essential, therefore, that you clearly articulate where you make a real difference – and this means developing crisp, clear and concise statements, ideally within just five or six words for each difference, with nothing flowery, fluffy or ambiguous.

6. **YOUR SIGNIFICANT ACHIEVEMENTS**
   (Now justify your claim above – Key Value-Adding Strengths)
   (Developed further in Chapter 7)

   For each Key Value-Adding Strength you identify, you must be able to provide at least six examples - indisputable evidence - that will justify your claim; and each example must be clearly and unambiguously presented, and ideally with supporting data.

   There is no point in making either loose or exaggerated claims of ability, skills etc. If you can't provide real evidence to support your claims, it is you who will appear as loose, fluffy, or ambiguous!

This is an area that challenges most people, mainly because they have been previously judged on either process, or completing a part within a series of actions; but it is the **end result** of your part in that process that needs to be drawn out!

7. **YOUR USP (UNIQUE SELLING PROPOSITION)**
Further developed in Chapter 8 – Personal Profiles.

Construct two paragraphs, each one no longer than four lines.

Paragraph 1: should position you perfectly for the role you aspire to, and summarise your skills, knowledge and experience.

It should, therefore, include your ideal next Job Title (from your Job Search Story); your Key Value-Adding Strengths, and the sectors you have experience of working in.

Paragraph 2: should summarise your key personal characteristics that enable you to do everything in the first paragraph so well. The easy way to develop this, is to condense what you have already created to answer the question in item three of this Chapter – What are you like at work?

An example of this might be:

Resilient and energetic **General Manager/Operations Director** *with a successful track record of driving down costs, improving operational performance and generating profitable business growth across a range of manufacturing industries: precision engineering, automotive, aerospace, electronics, fastenings, marine and construction.*

Combines a very flexible and collaborative nature with a clear communication style; and is recognised as a trusted partner working across all organisational levels to serve customers, business partners and other stakeholders. Acknowledged for bringing out the best in people, and going above and beyond to ensure the right results.

NB.
These two paragraphs will comfortably fit within four lines in an A4 format.

5.

Skills, Abilities and Competencies

vs

Key Value-Adding Strengths

The previous chapter introduced the concept of Key Value-Adding Strengths, as opposed to skills, but to ensure greater clarity the subject deserves more explanation to avoid confusion or misinterpretation as the terms are often used synonymously in the job searching/recruitment processes.

Skills and Abilities tend to be those aptitudes learned through training and may also be confirmed by qualification or certification/

diploma at an academic or functional training level. They can also be learned through repetition, or by following pre-determined processes, like computer-coding.

Competencies, as you will see on the following pages, are more about personal attributes – those character traits that show you act, rather than what you do. You might like to use some of those in compiling your answer to Q3 in the previous section – what are you like at work?

Key Value-Adding Strengths, are what we can do by combining those skills, abilities and competencies and where we bring something special – the expertise that sets you apart from others with a similar skill base.

These demonstrate your real value to a prospective employer and therefore differentiate you as a key player - a specialist not a generalist in the job market.

Expected Competencies

Despite many interviews demanding evidence of specific competencies, the reality is that few of those competencies are considered important enough to justify reward and therefore, as you won't be paid for them, you bring them for nothing!

They are, though, important enough to be part of the justification for making the appointment, so they are not to be ignored, but it is essential to understand that they are expected to exist in the person appointed, so don't claim them if you cannot justify them!

PERSONAL

Adaptability	Maintains effectiveness in a changing environment.
Commitment	Adds value and puts company before self-interest.
Compliance	Conforms to organisational politics.
Decisiveness	Makes decisions, judgments and takes action.
Energy	Maintains drive and directs high-level activity.
Flexibility	Modifies approach and style to gain objectives.
Independence	Has confidence in own convictions.
Initiative	Influences events, seeks opportunities, originates.
Integrity	Is honest, trustworthy and reliable.
Resilience	Remains effective despite disappointment/rejection.
Risk-taking	Calculates benefits against possible loss.
Self-motivated	Seeks satisfaction and demonstrable success.
Stress Tolerance	Maintains performance in pressure situations.
Tenacity	Sticking to a problem until solution achieved.
Vision	Focus on whole picture as the major objective.
Work Standards	Maintains standards for self and subordinates.

INTERPERSONAL

Listening	Receives and reacts to oral information.
Leading	Leads others and teams to achieve common goals.
Delegating	Effectively controls subordinates and resources.
Sociability	Mixes and participates easily with others effectively.
Persuasiveness	Gains support for own policies, ideas or viewpoint.
Teamwork	Creates desire in others to achieve common goals.
Sensitivity	Is conscious of needs of others.
Communication	Express things clearly and effectively
Motivating	Encourages individuals and circumstances.

ORGANISATIONAL

Planning	Establishes effective plans to achieve objectives.
Development	Maximises skills and competencies of subordinates.
Awareness	Is aware of broader effect of decisions or actions.
Environmental	Understands changing social and economic factors.
Structural Design	Creates effective corporate structures.

DECISION MAKING

Analysis	Identifies solutions from research and data analysis.
Creativity	Develops innovative and creative solutions.
Entrepreneurial	Takes opportunities to improve profitability.
Judgement	Uses logical assumptions and factual information.
Vision	Focuses on the macro rather than micro issues

PEOPLE

Addressing
Advising
Appraising
Assessing
Chairing Meetings
Coaching
Communicating:
- (briefing)
- (telephone)
- (written)
Controlling
Co-ordinating
Counselling
Decision Making
Delegating
Demonstrating
Developing
Directing
Empathising
Encouraging
Evaluating
Guiding
Helping
Illustrating
Influencing
Instructing
Interviewing
Leading
Liaising
Listening
Managing
Mediating
Monitoring
Motivating
Negotiating
Observing
Ordering
Organising

Persuading
Presenting
Proposing
Recommending
Recruiting
Representing
Selling
Setting Objectives
Supervising
Teaching
Team-building
Training

IDEAS/DATA

Adapting
Analysing
Anticipating
Appraising
Arranging
Assessing
Budgeting
Classifying
Collating
Composing
Conceiving
Creating
Defining
Designing
Developing
Devising
Editing
Eliminating
Establishing
Evaluating
Forecasting
Identifying
Initiating
Interpreting
Investigating

Itemising
Learning
Memorising
Organising
Outlining
Planning
Problem-solving
Processing
Producing
Promoting
Publicising
Recording
Reducing
Refining
Reorganising
Researching
Reviewing
Simplifying
Summarising
Synthesising
Testing
Translating
Unifying
Verifying
Visualising

PROJECTS

Achieving Targets
Adapting
Administering
Arranging
Combining
Controlling
Co-ordinating
Decision-making
Defining
Delivering
Designing
Despatching

Developing
Devising
Directing
Documenting
Eliminating
Establishing
Evaluating
Expanding
Experimenting
Generating
Implementing
Improvising
Innovating
Launching
Leading
Making Presentations
Managing
Modernising
Monitoring
Organising
Planning
Problem-solving
Producing
Refining
Reorganising
Researching
Resolving
Scheduling
Setting objectives
Simplifying
Streamlining
Trouble-shooting
Verifying
Working to deadlines
Working under pressure

6.

Your Key Value-Adding Strengths

(Where do you add particular Value?)

Whatever your functional role or seniority, the difference between what an organisation might EXPECT from any employee and what they truly VALUE clearly establishes what you might be worth to them.

An employer doesn't need you or pay you because you have:

- Communication Skills
- Presentation Skills
- Numeracy Skills
- Computer Skills
- Team Working Skills
- Listening Skills
- Flexibility or Adaptability
- Loyalty and Commitment

But might, because of what you can do with these skills!

Academic studies develop knowledge and basic abilities, but your value to an employer is in what you can actually achieve for them.

Our culture does not encourage or make you feel comfortable with 'selling yourself', but you can't leave it for others to work out!

You must be able to articulate what it is that makes you the perfect candidate, even though you might never have been encouraged to think in value-adding terms before and have difficulty articulating them.

Clearly however, without basic knowledge or ability, your capability to do the job you are paid to do would be severely limited. The reality is therefore that you bring these basic 'abilities' to the job for nothing - you are not paid for them.

You are paid for the difference you can make with them and that is your real VALUE.

The challenge, however, is that employees are rarely or never encouraged to identify their real Value-Adding Strengths, especially when organisations continue to label 'abilities' as 'skills'. The approach therefore calls for a different mind-set.

Your Key Value-adding Strengths are much stronger if they can be communicated in five words or fewer and presented in terms of:

Key Value-Adding Strengths

- Driving Organisational Performance
- Transforming Commercial Profitability
- Managing Key Stakeholder Relationships
- Delivering NPD and Innovation
- Transforming IT Service Delivery
- Improving Capacity and Quality
- Reducing Operational Costs
- Optimising Sales Value
- Driving Strategic Growth Strategies

Or:

Key Value-Adding Strengths Areas

- Compliance and Risk Management
- Health, Safety and Environment
- Campaign/Event Management
- Business Continuity and Disaster Recovery
- Organisational Performance and Profitability
- Recruitment, Retention and Development

NB: Most people only excel in just three or four key areas and only very rarely five. If you find yourself listing more, ask yourself if you would pay anyone for them – and beware - they only count if you can provide at least six compelling achievements to justify each them! See Chapter 7!

7.

Your Significant Achievements

(Now justify your Key Value-Adding Strengths!)

It is absolutely critical that you're able to provide indisputable evidence that will justify the Key Value-Adding Strengths you claim to have.

You must therefore produce at least six examples for each Key Value-Adding Strength. Try to use examples that are particularly relevant to the position sought.

Each example should ultimately be presented in a single bullet-pointed paragraph of no more than three lines. Your example should start with the end result, outcome, or measurable benefits to the organisation, eg, cost savings; performance improvements; increased profits etc; followed by what you actually did to achieve it.

In a culture where we tend to criticise more than affirm, we find it easier to highlight our limitations than articulate our strengths and achievements. Most people are uncomfortable when having to provide examples of what they have done, citing difficulty in 'selling themselves' or 'blowing their own trumpet' as it conflicts with a deeply held belief that it is wrong to brag or claim you are better than others.

Yet when job searching we are expected to demonstrate how good we are, so we need to be able to do it – with confidence and without embarrassment. If you can't tell people, they can't be expected to know!

Sometimes, if you've had difficulty identifying your Key Value-Adding Strengths, a way forward is to make a list of the key things you have done: projects you have been involved in, problems or challenges you've overcome, or activities that would have failed if you hadn't been there.

Just create a list of them – you can't have got to where you are in life without having done something! Then try grouping them into similar subject groups which may then identify key value-adding strengths you weren't even aware of!

You might even find out that you're better than you ever thought!

Then consider how you might explain each example using the acronym STAR:

S - What was the situation before you did anything with it?
T - What was the task that you were set or decided to deliver?
A - What were the key actions you took to resolve the issue?
R - What was the result, saving, improvement, outcome or benefit? Try to articulate these in measurable terms – finance/values, improvement levels/speed etc.

This information can also be used at interview, so rehearse what you've said; after all it is the truth as you have described it. Presenting some well thought-through facts is not at all embarrassing, so you will be able to use them with confidence.

The next step, is to simply turn each statement round into a format that can be even more useful and powerful to use in your CV. You will appreciate that organisations are actually more interested in Results and Actions you took to achieve them, than the fine details of process.

R - The Result
A - The Actions you took

This will then enable you to write each example up as a three-line, bullet pointed paragraph that can be transferred into your CV – making your presentation more powerful and as such, might attract more interest and discussion at interview – for which you will already be prepared.

For example: the following will fit comfortably on three lines at A4 size)

- Transformed a $12.5m loss (2015) into a $2.7m profit in 2017, by changing from a 50% market share with low margins, into an 18% market share with profitable margins, whilst retaining the most important customer relationships.

The following pages, with a detailed matrix and accompanying guidelines, together with additional pages of powerful verbs and a Thesaurus, will help you to correctly structure your own achievement paragraphs!

GUIDELINES TO SIMPLIFY COMPLETING THE ACHIEVEMENTS MATRIX

These guidelines will make writing your achievements an easier process. Follow them closely and they will really help. There are no shortcuts or alternatives.

STEP 1 – Heading: Prepare a sheet for each Key Value-Adding Strength and write that strength at the top where indicated.

STEP 2 – Example: Now identify the six very best examples you can think of that you could use to demonstrate your exceptional ability with that Key Value-Adding Strength. You only need to put a note in that column to remind you of what the example is – could be XYZ Project – keep them simple.

STEP 3 – Situation: Briefly explain what was happening BEFORE you were involved with it.

STEP 4 – Task: Briefly explain what you were asked or tasked to do, or that you decided to deliver on.

STEP 5 – Actions: Briefly explain the key actions that you took – keep them high level and avoid the temptation to add in unnecessary fluffy information – the matrix is tight on space to force you to focus on the key things you did, not everything you did!

STEP 6 – Result: Briefly again, state the end result, outcome or key benefit for the business. If not sure, chase it further by asking yourself 'which meant that ....' And when you've got that, ask yourself again 'which meant that .....'!

NB: Organisations are notorious for not encouraging their people to recognise and articulate the ultimate value of the work they have been doing. Sometimes, therefore, people get caught into thinking that 'process' is the end result. The real result, however, is the VALUE of the work delivered for the organisation, either in money saved, profit generated, or in performance/service improvement.

People sometimes struggle with this exercise for two reasons:

1. They don't follow the guidelines. Some think they don't need to follow them as they appear to be so easy, or think they know a better way. However 25 years' experience of using this tells me that there are no shortcuts and no alternative ways to getting it right!

2. They have never truly recognised the Outcome, Result, Value, or Benefit of what they have done - as far as the organisation is concerned!!

So to clarify, the result is the final outcome of the work you did. It is not a continuing part of the process, but the end – the ultimate benefit to the organisation.

It is not sufficient to say that the end result was the establishment of a new system, policy or procedure – the real end result is actually the commercial benefit of having that new system, policy or procedure in place.

Ultimately, this information will be cut and pasted into your CV – so it is absolutely key that the work you do here is high quality. Compromising on quality ultimately means you might compromise the quality of your CV.

It may feel like an uncomfortable and time-consuming process, but I promise you, the end result is worth it!

The examples on the following Achievement Matrix show how straightforward this exercise should be.

Please note though that the examples shown actually relate to three different Key Value-Adding Strengths; and you need to identify six examples for each Key Value-Adding Strength you claim to have.

EXAMPLE	SITUATION	TASK	ACTION	RESULT
KEY VALUE-ADDING STRENGTH: [examples below relate to different key value-adding strengths]				
Just a few words that remind you of the subject, example, or project	In a few words, what was happening before you got hold of it.	Again, in just a few words, what was the task you accepted, or decided to set for yourself.	Highlight your key or major actions that influenced the way forward - what were the most important things you did that enabled you to change the outcome.	What was the measurable end result for the organisation - then ask yourself the question 'which meant that ....' to make sure you get to the real outcome, benefit or result.
Culture Change	Old style manufacturing culture had no focus on customer service and potential new business was being lost to competitors	Turn the business into one that customers would be inspired to buy from	Led a significant culture change and training programme to secure employee buy in. Drove a total site clean up programme; introduced employee suggestions. Invited potential customers to visit	Increased turnover by 8% - £540k (£6.7m to £7.24m) and profits by 16% - £205k (£1.28m to £1.48m)
Relocating Manufacturing Operations	End of commercial lease and downturn in business volume, demanded that we find a lower cost operating base.	Find the most suitable and cost effective new location for manufacturing; and minimise all costs.	Identified alternative locations; negotiated realistic medium to long-term rental terms; created detailed planning, layout and moving processes; and secured employee commitment to making it happen on time and without affecting quality or service standards.	Reduced expected factory relocation costs by £265k - 41.5% (£638k down to £373k); and reduced annual overheads by £1.35m.
Partnership Arrangement	Innovation of clearly differentiated products had stalled	Drive greater NPD, innovation and deliver high quality products to market quicker	Developed partnerships with 16 Far East manufacturers of finished goods; forged close working links with their NPD people. Restablished the brand as one at the leading edge of technological innovation.	Bought 8 new products to market in 9 months, with potential additional sales of £1.35m per annum - and a projected year 5 figure of £7.3m

Strong Action Verbs To Power-Up Your CV

A

Absorbed
Accelerated
Accomplished
Accrued
Accumulated
Achieved
Acquired
Activated
Adapted
Addressed
Adjusted
Administered
Adopted
Advanced
Advised
Altered
Analysed
Announced
Anticipated
Applied
Appointed
Appraised
Approved
Arbitrated
Arranged
Ascertained
Assembled
Assessed
Assigned
Assisted
Attained
Attracted
Audited
Augmented
Authorised
Averted

Avoided
Awarded

B

Balanced
Bargained
Benefitted
Bolstered
Boosted
Bought
Broadened
Brought
Budgeted
Built

C

Calculated
Captured
Catalogued
Centralised
Changed
Checked
Coached
Collated
Collected
Combined
Communicated
Compiled
Completed
Composed
Conceived
Conducted
Consolidated
Constructed
Controlled
Converted
Co-ordinated

Corrected
Counselled
Created

D

Dealt with
Debated
Decided
Decreased
Defined
Delegated
Delivered
Demonstrated
Deployed
Designed
Despatched
Detailed
Detected
Determined
Developed
Devised
Diagnosed
Directed
Discovered
Dismantled
Dispensed
Displayed
Distributed
Diversified
Diverted
Documented
Doubled
Drafted

E

Earned
Edited

Educated
Effected
Elected
Eliminated
Empowered
Employed
Enacted
Encouraged
Ended
Enforced
Engineered
Enhanced
Enlarged
Enlisted
Ensured
Eradicated
Established
Estimated
Evaded
Evaluated
Examined
Exceeded
Excelled
Executed
Expanded
Expedited
Experimented
Explained
Exposed
Extended
Extracted

F

Facilitated
Finalised
Financed
Finished
Followed-
    through
Followed-up

Forecasted
Foresaw
Formed
Formulated
Fostered
(relationships)
Founded
Fulfilled
Furnished

G

Gained
Generated
Governed
Granted
Guaranteed
Guarded
Guided

H

Halted
Handled
Halved
Headed
Heightened
Helped
Highlighted
Hired
Hosted

I

Identified
Illustrated
Implemented
Improvised
Improved
Increased
Indexed
Influenced
Informed

Initiated
Innovated
Inspected
Inspired
Installed
Instigated
Instituted
Instructed
Integrated
Interpreted
Interviewed
Introduced
Invented
Invested
Investigated
Itemised

J

Judged
Juggled
Justified

L

Launched
Learned
Lectured
Led
Lengthened
Lessened
Liaised
Lightened
Liquidated
Listed
Listened
Logged
Lowered

M

Made
Maintained

Managed
Mapped
Marketed
Manipulated
Matched
Maximised
Measured
Mechanised
Mediated
Memorised
Mentored
Merged
Met
Minimised
Mitigated
Modelled
Modernised
Modified
Modulated
Monitored
Motivated
Moulded
Mounted
Multiplied

N

Navigated
Negotiated
Nominated

O

Observed
Obtained
Offered
Opened
Operated
Optimised
Ordered
Organised
Originated

Outlined
Overcome
Oversaw

P

Painted
Participated
Perceived
Performed
Persuaded
Piloted
Pinpointed
Pioneered
Planned
Positioned
Predicted
Prepared
Prescribed
Presented
Presided
Prevented
Probed
Problem-solved
Processed
Procured
Produced
Programmed
Projected
Promoted
Proposed
Protected
Proved
Provided
Publicised
Published
Purchased

Q

Qualified
Quantified

Questioned
Quoted

R

Raised
Reacted
Read
Realigned
Realised
Re-arranged
Reasoned
Received
Recognised
Recommended
Reconciled
Reconstructed
Recorded
Recovered
Recruited
Rectified
Redeployed
Redesigned
Redirected
Reduced
Referred
Refined
Reformed
Regenerated
Regulated
Rehabilitated
Reinforced
Reinstated
Rejected
Rejuvenated
Related
Released
Remedied
Remodelled
Rendered
Renegotiated

Renewed
Renovated
Reorganised
Repaired
Replaced
Reported
Represented
Rescued
Researched
Resolved
Responded
Restored
Restructured
Restyled
Retained
Retrieved
Revamped
Reversed
Reviewed
Revised
Revitalised
Revived
Revolutionised

S

Salvaged
Satisfied
Saved
Scheduled
Screened
Secured
Segmented
Served
Serviced
Selected
Separated
Settled
Set-up
Shaped
Shared

Shortened
Showed
Sketched
Skilled
Simplified
Sold
Solved
Sorted
Sparked
Specified
Spurred
Stabilised
Staffed
Standardised
Started
Steered
Stemmed
Stimulated
Stopped
Streamlined
Strengthened
Stretched
Structured
Studied
Submitted
Succeeded
Suggested
Summarised
Superintended
Supervised
Supplemented
Supplied
Supported
Surpassed
Sustained
Surveyed
Synthesised

T

Tailored
Taught

Tendered
Terminated
Tested
Tightened
Traced
Tracked
Traded
Trained
Transcribed
Transferred
Transformed
Transitioned
Translated
Transposed
Travelled
Trimmed
Tripled
Turned around

U

Uncovered
Undertook
Unified
United
Unravelled
Updated
Urged
Upgraded
Utilised

V

Vacated
Validated
Verbalised
Verified
Vetted
Viewed
Visited
Vitalised

W

Weighed
Widened
Withdrew
Withstood
Witnessed
Won
Worked
Wrote

Thesaurus:
Alternative Words To Power-Up Your CV

MANAGED AND CONTROLLED	PROCURED OR UTILISED	ORIGINATED OR STARTED
Authorised	Accrued	Appointed
Budgeted	Accumulated	Built
Controlled	Acquired	Conceived
Decided	Bought	Constructed
Delegated	Captured	Created
Determined	Collected	Devised
Directed	Employed	Established
Empowered	Enlisted	Founded
Headed	Gained	Generated
Influenced	Hired	Initiated
Instructed	Interviewed	Inspired
Led	Learned	Installed
Managed	Obtained	Instigated
Observed	Purchased	Instituted
Ordered	Recruited	Introduced
Oversaw	Retained	Invented
Persuaded	Secured	Launched
Piloted	Utilised	Originated
Presided		Piloted
Regulated		Pioneered
Staffed		Rejuvenated
Steered		Renewed
Superintended		Set-up
Supervised		Started
Taught		
Trained		

INCREASED / MADE BIGGER

Accelerated
Augmented
Broadened
Doubled
Enlarged
Exceeded
Expanded
Extended
Heightened
Increased
Lengthened
Maximised
Strengthened
Surpassed
Tripled
Widened

COMMUNICATED OR INFORMED

Communicated
Debated
Explained
Informed
Listened
Mediated
Renegotiated

PREPARED OR PLANNED

Administered
Arranged
Assembled
Centralised
Compiled
Composed
Co-ordinated
Deployed
Designed
Developed
Dismantled
Engineered
Mounted
Organised
Planned
Positioned
Prepared
Programmed
Proposed
Scheduled
Structured

PREVENTED OR ENDED

Anticipated
Assisted
Averted
Avoided
Completed
Diverted
Eliminated
Ended
Eradicated
Evaded
Finalised
Finished
Followed through
Followed up
Forestalled
Guarded
Halted
Liquidated
Prevented
Rejected
Stemmed
Stopped
Terminated

SUCCEEDED OR ACHIEVED	RESEARCHED OR STUDIED	IMPROVED PERFORMANCE
Accomplished	Analysed	Corrected
Achieved	Appraised	Enhanced
Attained	Assessed	Improved
Completed	Audited	Optimised
Ensured	Calculated	Rectified
Negotiated	Catalogued	Refined
Overcame	Checked	Remedied
Recognised	Collated	Repaired
Saved	Defined	Rescued
Secured	Diagnosed	Resolved
Succeeded	Discovered	Restored
Surpassed	Estimated	Revised
Traded	Evaluated	Revitalised
Won	Examined	Revived
	Exposed	Revolutionised
	Extracted	Saved
	Highlighted	Solved
	Identified	Transformed
	Indexed	Unravelled
	Inspected	
	Investigated	
	Memorised	
	Monitored	
	Probed	
	Proved	
	Reconciled	
	Reported	
	Researched	
	Reviewed	
	Revised	
	Studied	
	Summarised	
	Surveyed	
	Tested	
	Traced	
	Uncovered	
	Verified	

CHANGED OR ALTERED

Adjusted
Altered
Changed
Combined
Converted
Diversified
Juggled
Mechanised
Modernised
Modified
Moulded
Rearranged
Redeployed
Redesigned
Redirected
Reorganised
Renovated
Replaced
Restructured
Shaped
Simplified
Sold
Streamlined
Tightened
Transferred
Transformed
Unified
United
Vitalised

LESSENED OR REDUCED

Decreased
Halved
Lessened
Lightened
Lowered
Minimised
Mitigated
Reduced
Shortened
Trimmed

PREPARED

Documented
Drafted
Edited
Interpreted
Outlined
Publicised
Published
Revamped
Revised
Translated

PROGRESSED OR CHASED

Activated
Coached
Dealt With
Despatched
Encouraged
Facilitated
Foresaw
Fostered
(Relationships)
Helped
Inspired
Motivated
Spurred
Stimulated
Taught
Trained
Urged

MAINTAINED

Consolidated
Maintained
Regulated
Reinforced
Retained
Settled
Stabilised
Standardised
Supported

OBTAINED OR USED

Accrued
Accumulated
Acquired
Bought
Captured
Collected
Employed
Enlisted
Gained
Hired
Interviewed
Learned
Obtained
Purchased
Recruited
Retained
Secured

IMPLEMENTED OR ACTIONED

Applied
Conducted
Demonstrated
Effected
Enacted
Enforced
Executed
Formed
Formulated
Implemented
Marketed
Merged
Modulated
Negotiated
Operated
Participated
Perceived
Performed
Presented
Problem-Solved
Processed
Procured
Produced
Projected
Provided
Related
Released
Rendered
Represented
Serviced
Sorted
Synthesised
Travelled
Undertook
Utilised
Viewed
Visited

SUGGESTED OR ADVISED

Advised
Approved
Counselled
Forecast
Guided
Judged
Liaised
Prescribed
Promoted
Proposed
Recommended
Selected
Specified
Suggested

8.

Creating Your CV

Why Most CVs Fall Short of The Mark

Despite the impact of technology and some organisations' continued reliance on the use of Application Forms, there is still a need for a good CV – where you can control the content, the way it is presented, and its impact on potential employers.

Its importance in your job search should never be under-estimated.

The multitude of CVs received by companies and recruiters daily, clearly demonstrate that they are nothing more than a brain dump of information, or even a compilation of regurgitated and sometimes unrelated job descriptions.

Most CV's are constructed without the writer having a clear appreciation of their importance, how they are read and without clear focus on the role it is being directed towards. Many people merely copy one of the multitude of templates available on the internet; and don't take any specialist advice or guidance that would make it more effective.

CVs tend to be presented in either the hope or expectation that someone, somewhere, will take the time and trouble to wade through it, find something of interest in it; understand what isn't in it, or indeed correctly interpret what is.

Many 'CV Guide Books' instruct the reader to create a CV that matches the requirements of the job they are applying for; and whilst the instruction is given with the best intentions, it leaves the job seeker with the belief that they should be creating a new CV for each application and/or that their CV should look like the job description of the job they are applying for!

Experience shows the value of having a well-written CV that clearly demonstrates to the reader why that person should be considered to be a worthy applicant for the role in question, without having to try and work out why!

You Must Make Your CV Even Better!

Your CV is your marketing tool - your advert - and is the information on which a recruiter or employer will make a decision to see you - or not. It must therefore be about you, not just anybody who has done similar jobs to you; and it must stand up to close scrutiny – so no lies!!

Recruiters receive many hundreds of CVs each day and are known to filter them after scanning through them for only seven - ten seconds each. It is therefore essential that you commit the time, effort and energy to make sure your CV does the job you need it to do - effectively.

It must, therefore, deliver your potential value to them, presenting your key qualifications, key value-adding strengths, knowledge, experience, career history and achievements, together with your personality - but it is not your life story!

It is not just a history of where you have been - with the responsibilities of each job listed like a job description. Prospective employers need to be impressed by your results - the benefits you have delivered before so they can understand the value you can now bring to them.

It should present you - your relevant and important information - in a way that will create an enthusiasm and expectation that you could be the right candidate for them; and be encouraged to invite you to interview.

Presentation must be business style – factual and with no punctuation errors or spelling mistakes. You do not want your errors to define you. It should be kept to a maximum of three pages and be easy for the reader to scan/read.

NB Recruiters will also use your CV as an 'aide memoire' or reference tool during the interview process, so it is important that you remember what you have included - and why!

YOUR CV

What You Should Include or Ensure

- Your name should be the largest font on the page – with your first name being the one you want people to use at interview – you are not called Mr, Mrs or Ms, you are a real person!

- Your contact information including your address – remember that withholding information might give the potential recruiter reason for wondering why, and that might keep you off their 'first choice' list.

- Write in the third person and past tense so that each of your statements will be seen as fact and not opinions. Using third person verbs eg. 'managed' is much more powerful than 'I managed'.

- Relevant qualifications, skills and experience, with real evidence –your achievements and delivered benefits in quantifiable financial or percentage terms, or as time/volume improvements.

- An overview of your career history with dates in just years – not the months as well – and it should have no gaps, or interviewers will be asking questions about the gaps and not the content!

- It should be written with positive factual statements, but not opinions – neither yours nor other people's; and it should help the reader to appreciate your worth, not have to try to work that out!

- It should convey your personality, character, working-style, motivations, and attitude that shows what it is about you that has enabled you to achieve so many things.

- If printing hard copies, choose a good quality white paper – there is still a perceived connection between high quality information and the quality of the paper stock it is printed on.

Remember

- Your CV is your marketing tool – it has to work for you in your absence. Don't expect the reader to take time to work out whether you are an ideal candidate, or potential organisational asset.

- You must, at worst, make it really difficult for them to easily discard you, so make your CV do the work you need it to do – and then stand up – stand out – and stand firmly at the front of the queue!

What You Should Avoid or Leave Out

- Don't use Curriculum Vitae as a heading; it's both unnecessary and old fashioned – we know it's a CV and you don't head letters with the word Letter in similar circumstances, for the same reason!

- Avoid spelling or grammatical errors, especially if you're used to using small space messaging systems like Text or Twitter – this is a business document and you want to be perceived as good.

- Avoid elaborate presentation styles – no fancy covers, folders or binders, or visual effects – recruiters just don't have time to deal with them. They are a distraction and likely to be a reason to reject you.

- No previous company logos, diagrams or photographs as they are an unnecessary visual distraction. Your CV is about you and your credibility must be greater than the companies you've worked for.

- Avoid boxes, shading and obscure fonts that the recipient might not have on their computer. Your CV has to work both on screen and on paper; and through electronic Applicant Tracking Systems.

- Avoid abbreviations or jargon wherever possible – you might have had a common 'internal language' that covered equipment or processes, but the reader probably won't understand it!

- Don't include current/anticipated salary package, non-essential personal information like: marital status, children's names/ages, height, weight, state of health, or religious/political beliefs.

- Don't include referees' names or contact details. They are regarded as clutter on your CV – and recruiters will not want to interview you just because you've got references available!

- Do not state the reasons for leaving each job – whilst you may be asked to explain why at interview, your reason for leaving is never likely to be a positive reason for interviewing you.

- Adding copies of qualification certificates, even though they may be requested later in the selection process, will merely clutter your CV and irritate the potential recipient – they don't have the time!

- There is really no need to include school examination results that are superceded by higher qualifications – these are included by those who have nothing positive to say and are trying to fill space!

Personal Profiles

This is one of the most challenging parts of creating a CV - most profiles are totally useless - they are generic, show no real value and could be about just anyone, at any level – and often not the person in the CV!

To better understand the challenge, it is important to look at some of the profiles in use and ask yourself whether you would really bother to look at them; whether you would really know anything important or valuable about the individual; and would you believe anything in them!

See for yourself – they could be anybody, at almost any level in any functional discipline, from either the public or private sector. They do not help the reader to know the level they are at, what value-adding expertise they bring, or the sector/s they are experienced in.

WARNING: VERY POOR PERSONAL PROFILES –
Do Not Copy!

A senior, multi-skilled, commercially aware manager with a proven track record of the development and management of cross-departmental projects or teams.

I am professional, hardworking, enthusiastic and innovative; and have excellent communication skills and work well either individually or in a team. I seek out where improvements can be made and work co-operatively with others to develop services.

A creative thinker with a reputation for resolving difficult and complex commercial issues. A driving force for change, improvement and delivery in a wide range of business activities and cultures. Recognised as an excellent, experienced negotiator.

Commercial, customer focused Chartered Accountant with strong Business Partnering background supported by excellent technical, analytical and people skills combined with a mastery of systems and processes.

GOOD PERSONAL PROFILES

A good personal profile is your clear marketing statement. It is a summary that positions you in the mind of the reader, so they can decide whether you – out of hundreds of other candidates – are worthy of being invited to interview. Good personal profiles do work!

We know that recruiters only take seven to ten seconds to look at your CV initially to determine whether you might be of interest – and then only one to two minutes more to make their decision before inviting the shortlisted candidates to interview. A good profile should be you – at your best!

Your personal profile must therefore, enable the reader to clearly see why you are a worthy candidate for a role they may be seeking to fill, or for a challenge they need to resolve. You cannot expect, or even hope, the reader will take longer over your CV than others; nor that they will be able to work out what strengths you might bring, or what valuable contribution you might make. Remember, if you don't tell them, they won't know!

So your profile must tell the reader what functional role you are suited to, what level you are at – Director or Senior Manager – what value-adding strengths you can bring, and what sectors/ environments you are experienced in. Good genuine personal profiles make you stand out!

At the same time, it is also essential that the reader has an opportunity to appreciate your working style – the way you work and how you actually achieve everything you do! A good quality profile shows you at your best!

This may sound like a very tall order – but if you look back to Chapter 4 – Presentation Statements – part five encourages you to create two paragraphs – the first that positions you perfectly for the role you aspire to; and the second that summarises your key personal characteristics.

The next pages demonstrate what a good personal profile is – see how the reader will be made aware of the quality of the person in it!

But beware! They are examples and not to be copied, as they are not written by you, for you, or about you. **You must create your own!**

EXAMPLE PROFILE PARAGRAPHS

Please note that each of the following paragraphs will comfortably fit on 3 lines in an A4 size document.

Valued and innovative **Technical Director**, proven in driving global satellite-based tracking technologies and other leading edge electronics. Delivers key complex projects, develops new global business growth and secures multi-national approvals within niche, and forward-thinking businesses across a broad range of advanced technology-focused environments.

Acknowledged for achieving exceptional results by transforming organisations and teams to deliver efficiency and high standards. Quickly inspires momentum, commitment and best practice within optimised systems and processes. Fosters honest and open collaboration, recognised for direct, precise communication, concise decision-making and patient logic.

A fastidiously organised and driven **Production Director**, skilled in optimising performance, minimising waste; and driving both plant capacity and reliability. Improves health and safety performance, and establishes best practice compliance. Optimises strategic performance in high volume, high value and specialty chemicals in highly regulated medical environments.

Applies a pragmatic approach to developing detailed action plans. Promotes the belief that an inclusive environment, with appropriate motivation and development, optimises people's capabilities and creates the high-performing teams that drive overall business success. Recognised for building strong internal and external networks, based on mutual trust.

Highly experienced **European HR Specialist**, skilled in developing robust Pan-European HR strategies and harmonising operating structures. Drives key initiatives and projects within the complexities of international mergers, acquisitions and divestments. Acknowledged as a valuable, credible and ethical Board member.

Recognised for a consultative management style - guiding subordinates, encouraging others to share views and opinions, and promoting individual and group development. Respected by both Board and peer groups for expecting high standards, working across the business, and promoting multi-departmental teams to achieve collaborative goals.

Highly acclaimed **Managing Director**, proven in delivering profitable and sustainable growth in specialist medical/electronic appliance markets. Builds strong partnership relationships with manufacturers, distributor networks, and key retailers. Delivers highly effective business, people and innovation strategies; and develops robust key stakeholder partnerships.

Recognised for being a very task-focused leader, expecting the highest levels of quality from teams, and generating a right first time attitude. Develops robust working relationships with professional advisors and financial institutions, supported by personal credibility and a strong track record. Appreciated for empowering others and encouraging them to excel.

Commercially focused **Group Finance Director**, particularly valued in supporting both Board and stakeholder strategies, maintaining corporate governance and business integrity; and securing the profitability, efficiency and cash generation of B2B service and technology organisations. Acknowledged as a highly respected and trusted advisor.

An approachable and systematic professional with an uncompromising passion for the brand, products and people. Combines a pragmatic, analytical and focused drive that inspires a will to deliver with clear strategic and tactical guidelines. Creates a robust operating culture with a clear vision and direction, that encourages loyalty and a genuine shared sense of purpose.

Different CV Styles

In principle there are just 3 main styles of CV:

- Reverse Chronological
- Hybrid of the Reverse Chronological and Functional
- Functional

And the key difference between them is the structure of the first page.

THE REVERSE CHRONOLOGICAL CV

- Easiest to prepare – it is the 'traditional style' and most used.
- Emphasises the most recent job title, employer, and time in role.
- Lists all positions held, by date, working backwards from current or latest position.
- May be useful when your career history and next position follows a natural course of progression through specialist role or industry.

However
- Likely to be received as a typical CV - just like everyone else's.
- May contain many repetitions of actions/achievements through a series of functional roles.
- Your suitability or potential could be judged just by your last job title or organisation.
- It leaves the reader to identify your value if they even take the trouble to work that out.

First Name and Surname

Full address including Postcode
Tel: 12345 678901   **Mobile: 01234 567890**
E-mail: ????????@yourisp.com   LinkedIn: www.linkedin.com/123456

Resilient and energetic **General Manager/Operations Director,** acknowledged for driving down costs, improving operational performance and generating profitable business growth. Delivers critical 'lean' improvements to transform the performance of precision engineering, automotive, aerospace, electronics, fastenings, marine and construction businesses.

A determined and goal-orientated strategist, with proven leadership and motivational skills demonstrated in both unionised and non-unionised environments. Inspires individuals and teams to achieve personal and organisational goals that deliver sustainable business growth through change management programmes and Continuous Improvement cultures.

QUALIFICATIONS

MBA - Graduate Business School.
B.Sc. Tech. (Hons) in The Science and Technology of Materials.
BSc Computation, University of Manchester Institute of Science and Technology **(UMIST)**

CAREER HISTORY

OPERATIONS DIRECTOR, A N Other Company   **2016 – to date**
£35m t/over manufacturer of precision engineered units for international markets, with 300 people. A dual site role operating in unionised environments with customers in Aerospace, Marine Diesel, Escalator, Conveyor, Automotive, Distribution and General Industrial Sectors.

- Reported direct to the UK Managing Director and responsible for all site P&L activities including manufacturing, sales, quality, engineering, materials management, procurement, maintenance and new product development.
- Increased UK t/over in 2 years, by 6.7% (from £43.6m to £46.5m) and gross profit by 16.7% (from £8.5m to £9.9m), by restructuring supply chain processes, challenging traditional 'we do it this way' mind sets and transforming shift structures.
- Took Eastern European profits from €1.5m to €2.2m in 2 years, by agreeing a brand licence with a manufacturing partner and opening a digital operation that optimised brand and profit opportunities on a broader scale.
- Generated an additional $2.5m profit over a projected 4 year period by renegotiating an £5.5m Asian contract that also allowed a local contract manufacturer to utilise the brand whilst ensuring consistency with the global brand and product range.
- Increased production by 47% (2400 to 3528 tpa) to protect a $4m supply contract. Reduced annual maintenance from 40 days to 22 and start-up snags from 3 weeks to just 2 days. Transformed engineering into a quality first time culture.
- Avoided the need for a $8.75m plant investment by increasing the capacity of existing plant by 22% (1800 to 2196 tpa). Optimised existing equipment, improved production planning and established longer production runs and fewer product changeovers.
- Ensured the continued production of a valuable 30,000 tonne pa pull-through product for Asian and European markets, preventing closure of a low profit site by proving operational viability with cost increases below the competition.
- Increased production by 47% (2400 to 3528 tpa) to protect a $4m supply contract. Reduced annual maintenance from 40 days to 22 and start-up snags from 3 weeks to just 2 days. Transformed engineering into a quality first time culture.
- Avoided the need for a $8.75m plant investment by increasing the capacity of existing plant by 22% (1800 to 2196 tpa). Optimised existing equipment, improved production planning and established longer production runs and fewer product changeovers.

THE HYBRID CV

- This is an adaption of the reverse chronological CV and inserts some key skills and brief explanation before the listing of jobs.

- It is relatively easy to produce but still tends to lean towards your value being judged by your previous job title and/or organisation.

- It might also be used by those in highly technical areas – like IT – where hardware and software systems' experience might be particularly important to highlight.

First Name and Surname
Full address including Postcode
Tel: 12345 678901   **Mobile: 01234 567890**
E-mail: ????????@yourisp.com   LinkedIn: www.linkedin.com/123456

Resilient and energetic **General Manager/Operations Director,** acknowledged for driving down costs, improving operational performance and generating profitable business growth. Delivers critical 'lean' improvements to transform the performance of precision engineering, automotive, aerospace, electronics, fastenings, marine and construction businesses.

A determined and goal-orientated strategist, with proven leadership and motivational skills demonstrated in both unionised and non-unionised environments. Inspires individuals and teams to achieve personal and organisational goals that deliver sustainable business growth through change management programmes and Continuous Improvement cultures.

QUALIFICATIONS
MBA - Graduate Business School.
B.Sc. Tech. (Hons) in The Science and Technology of Materials.
BSc Computation, University of Manchester Institute of Science and Technology **(UMIST)**

KEY VALUE-ADDING STRENGTHS

DELIVERING PROFITABLE AND SUSTAINABLE GROWTH
- Increased UK t/over in 2 years, by 6.7% (from £43.6m to £46.5m) and gross profit by 16.7% (from £8.5m to £9.9m).

DRIVING MANUFACTURING EFFICIENCY AND REDUCING COSTS
- Increased production by 47% (2400 to 3528 tpa) reduced annual maintenance from 40 days to 22 and start-up snags from 3 weeks to just 2 days.

DELIVERING STRATEGIC BUSINESS AND PEOPLE INNOVATION
- Turned around an historic legacy of near fatal accidents by making this issue the key HSE priority.

CAREER HISTORY

OPERATIONS DIRECTOR, A N Other Company   **2016 – to date**
£35m t/over manufacturer of precision engineered units for international markets, with 300 people. A dual site role operating in unionised environments with customers in Aerospace, Marine Diesel, Escalator, Conveyor, Automotive, Distribution and General Industrial Sectors.

- Reported direct to the UK Managing Director and responsible for all site P&L activities including manufacturing, sales, quality, engineering, materials management, procurement, maintenance and new product development.
- Took Eastern European profits from €1.5m to €2.2m in 2 years, by agreeing a brand licence with a manufacturing partner and opening a digital operation that optimised brand and profit opportunities on a broader scale.
- Generated an additional $2.5m profit over a projected 4 year period by renegotiating an £5.5m Asian contract that also allowed a local contract manufacturer to utilise the brand whilst ensuring consistency with the global brand and product range.
- Increased production by 47% (2400 to 3528 tpa) to protect a $4m supply contract. Reduced annual maintenance from 40 days to 22 and start-up snags from 3 weeks to just 2 days. Transformed engineering into a quality first time culture.
- Avoided the need for a $8.75m plant investment by increasing the capacity of existing plant by 22% (1800 to 2196 tpa). Optimised existing equipment, improved production planning and established longer production runs and fewer product changeovers.

THE FUNCTIONAL CV

- Presents your value to prospective employers in a way that best reflects your preferred job target, by leading with your key value-adding strengths and making a very powerful impact.
- Emphasising and combining key value-adding strengths and achievements from a variety of roles will minimise the incidence of repetition and increase your power/value.

Advantages

- Has a more dynamic impact and provides an opportunity for you to be seen as different, better and more interesting than other candidates.
- When your career history has remained in one area of specialism and you need needs to demonstrate a broader capability than that indicated by your current job title.
- Particularly useful where your current role carries a less than clear title that would not be as recognisable outside of your current organisation.
- When your key transferable value-adding strengths are much more important than your career history to establish credibility or confirm suitability for a new/different role.
- Ensures that the reader is quickly drawn to the key value-adding strengths and accomplishments; and their alignment to the preferred role you seek.
- Presents greater value where breadth or depth of experience in any one role or function is limited. Minimises repetition and enables less-credible roles/assignments to be down played.

However

- It needs greater self-awareness and a clearer understanding of your preferred next job.
- It will seem lightweight if focused on abilities, traits and qualities instead of true value-adding strengths.

First Name and Surname
Full address including Postcode
Tel: 12345 678901   **Mobile: 01234 567890**
E-mail: ????????@yourisp.com   LinkedIn: www.linkedin.com/123456

Resilient and energetic **General Manager/Operations Director,** acknowledged for driving down costs, improving operational performance and generating profitable business growth. Delivers critical 'lean' improvements to transform the performance of precision engineering, automotive, aerospace, electronics, fastenings, marine and construction businesses.

A determined and goal-orientated strategist, with proven leadership and motivational skills demonstrated in both unionised and non-unionised environments. Inspires individuals and teams to achieve personal and organisational goals that deliver sustainable business growth through change management programmes and Continuous Improvement cultures.

QUALIFICATIONS

MBA - Graduate Business School.
B.Sc. Tech. (Hons) in The Science and Technology of Materials.
BSc Computation, University of Manchester Institute of Science and Technology **(UMIST)**

KEY VALUE-ADDING STRENGTHS

DELIVERING PROFITABLE AND SUSTAINABLE GROWTH

- Increased UK t/over in 2 years, by 6.7% (from £43.6m to £46.5m) and gross profit by 16.7% (from £8.5m to £9.9m), by restructuring supply chain processes, challenging traditional 'we do it this way' mind sets and transforming shift structures.
- Took Eastern European profits from €1.5m to €2.2m in 2 years, by agreeing a brand licence with a manufacturing partner and opening a digital operation that optimised brand and profit opportunities on a broader scale.
- Generated an additional $2.5m profit over a projected 4 year period by renegotiating an £5.5m Asian contract that also allowed a local contract manufacturer to utilise the brand whilst ensuring consistency with the global brand and product range.

DRIVING MANUFACTURING EFFICIENCY AND REDUCING COSTS

- Increased production by 47% (2400 to 3528 tpa) to protect a $4m supply contract. Reduced annual maintenance from 40 days to 22 and start-up snags from 3 weeks to just 2 days. Transformed engineering into a quality first time culture.
- Avoided the need for a $8.75m plant investment by increasing the capacity of existing plant by 22% (1800 to 2196 tpa). Optimised existing equipment, improved production planning and established longer production runs and fewer product changeovers.
- Ensured the continued production of a valuable 30,000 tonne pa pull-through product for Asian and European markets, preventing closure of a low profit site by proving operational viability with cost increases below the competition.

DELIVERING STRATEGIC BUSINESS AND PEOPLE INNOVATION

- Turned around an historic legacy of near fatal accidents working at height to low potential near misses by making this issue the key HSE priority. Near fatal incidents reduced to low potential within 1 year owing to technical and behavioural changes.
- Established best practise whilst integrating specialist environment teams, improving production by 20%, packing by 43% and reducing logistics failures by 15%. Mapped and harmonised working practises into value streams without compromising profits.
- Transformed silo departments into cross-functional teams based on category and consumer need, to create a common discipline between marketing and engineering; and ensure fit for purpose and on time delivery.

OPERATIONS DIRECTOR, A N Other Company   **2016 – to date**
£35m t/over manufacturer of precision engineered units for international markets, with 300 people. A dual site role operating in unionised environments with customers in Aerospace, Marine Diesel, Escalator, Conveyor, Automotive, Distribution and General Industrial Sectors.

- Reported direct to the UK Managing Director and responsible for all site P&L activities including manufacturing, sales, quality, engineering, materials management, procurement, maintenance and new product development.
- Turned around a business unit losing £1m per annum, and in 14 months achieved over £100K per month profits, by improving product availability and service levels on the more profitable segments of the product portfolio.
- Transformed a previous 'manufacturing' culture to one focused on product, brand and the consumer. Secured the buy-in of the entire workforce to share a common commitment to servicing customers better.
- Protected the organisation's reputation from inconsistent HSE risk assessment quality and detail. Simplified the process by standardising the questions in simple English and re-focused the process to look only at HSE risks and rank them accordingly.
- Restored organisational confidence in a production site with historic management and supply issues, ensuring that a block on investment was lifted. Replaced the entire management team and provided close support to ensure the new team's success.
- Achieved annualized cost savings of £2.2m by reducing raw material and component costs; and by rationalising organisational structures to introduce a more streamlined work flow and facilitate productivity improvements.
- Reduced inventory levels by over £3m by supply chain rationalisation, the introduction of finite capacity scheduling systems and process re-engineering.
- Increased factory output and productivity by 45% with new plant and equipment and Kaizen activities to remove bottlenecks. Reduced key manufacturing lead-times by up to 80% and working capital by £450K by managing a factory relay out project.
- Eliminated £1m/annum of fixed overhead by successfully integrating two manufacturing facilities into one without compromising customer service.
- Secured £2.5m/annum of new business by project managing the NPI, implementing TS16949 compliant systems and procedures and introducing 5S programmes.

OPERATIONS DIRECTOR, A Different Company   **2011 – 2016**
£17m t/over non-unionised manufacturer of products including gaskets, seals, service kits and sub-assemblies with 60 people offering design, make and supply chain management solutions to a variety of blue chip heating and automotive customers.

- Reported direct to the Managing Director and responsible for design, operations, quality, supply chain management and sales and marketing.
- Reduced inventories by £250k and labour costs by £135k/annum, by installing new production equipment and introducing a computerized bar coding system to manage customer Kanban stocks and improve delivery performance.
- Developed site best practise for safe recommissioning of assets post maintenance in process safety management led environment. Implemented new methodologies based on legacy systems with significant upgrading to meet current best practise
- Generated annualised cost savings of £100k by developing a new organisational structure to improve performance and communication.
- Overturned a "seriously deficient" audit rating to one judged "controlled" in 2 years. Redesigned the entire permit system, re-defined responsibilities within the system and removed contract companies that were unable to comply with new procedures.
- Secured £3m of revenue with ABD Automotive Systems by offering innovative solutions to supply chain logistics and pricing problems at the re-negotiation of contracts.
- Increased annual revenues by £4.2m and profitability by 20% in 2 years through the introduction of new products, improving component availability levels from 60% to 95%; and by driving the development and promotion of new products and services.

OPERATIONS DIRECTOR, Yet Another Company   **2006 – 2011**
£15m t/over automotive and electronics manufacturing business (subsidiary of a major Group) with 180 people (originally 232) operating in a unionised environment.

- Reported direct to the COO and responsible for all P & L activities including sales, marketing, engineering and operations, with a targeted expectation of significantly improving manufacturing performance.
- Improved manufacturing productivity by 35% (saving £900k p.a.). Reduced lead-time by 60% and working capital by £450K, by introducing lean manufacturing techniques and incentive schemes.
- Generated £800K of annualised cost savings and increased sales per employee by 30% by leading a restructuring programme that reduced headcount by fifty-two.
- Negotiated a three-year deal with a key international customer to secure £3m of revenue.

OPERATIONS DIRECTOR, Even More Company   **1998 - 2006**
An engineered components manufacturing business with a turnover of £18 million and 100 unionised employees (originally 153) operating on three different sites, including a foundry.

- Reported direct to the COO and responsible for all operational, business development and commercial activities.
- Increased revenues by £600k by driving the development and promotion of new products and services.
- Generated productivity improvements of up to 80% and annualised savings of £500k by introducing various incentive schemes and modern manufacturing techniques.
- Reduced casting costs by more than 55% or £250K and simplified the supply chain management issues in the process by sub-contracting foundry operations.
- Increased turnover per employee from £42K to £81K per annum.
- Reduced working capital inventory from £2.3m to £1.5m.

OPERATIONS MANAGER, A Very High Tech Company   **1995 – 1998**
An aftermarket manufacturer supplying markets in Europe, Asia and Africa with a turnover of £18m and 120 employees. A non-unionised organisation.

- Reported direct to the Plant Manager and responsible for new product design and introduction, development of quality systems, production, manufacturing engineering, Operational Excellence (6 Sigma), development of customer accounts and suppliers and contract negotiation.
- Increased sales revenue and profitability by 20% in two years by introducing new products and improving product availability levels from 60% to 95%.
- Reduced the costs of purchased components by £2m and improved supply for 80% (£4m) of them by appointing and supporting new subcontract component suppliers.

BUSINESS UNIT MANAGER, Another High Tech Company   **1993 – 1995**
Car parts manufacturer supplying all the major European Passenger Car and Commercial Diesel OEM's with a turnover of £80m and 700 unionised employees.

- Reported direct to the Plant Manager and responsible for all aspects of manufacturing activity for OEM customers, raw material procurement, scheduling, customer liaison, managing a workforce of 120 employees, maintenance of £5m of capital equipment.
- Increased output and labour efficiency by 60% for component manufacture.
- Reduced inventory and lead times by 80% by introducing One Piece Flow and JIT.

DESIGN/MANUFACTURING ENGR, Another High Tech Company   **1988 – 1993**
PROCESS DEVELOPMENT ENGINEER, My First Company   **1986 – 1988**

LEISURE INTERESTS
        Sport including rugby, football (refereeing), basketball, cricket and athletics; history and reading.

CV CONSTRUCTION GUIDELINES

The following simple, step-by-step guide will help you structure a strong and impactful CV.

1. Plan to keep your CV within an absolute maximum of three pages – the recruiter doesn't have the time or inclination to read any more and probably wouldn't even remember it if they did!
2. Use the images shown, to help position the information clearly and in a logical order, so you ensure the reader is presented with what you need them to know to raise interest in you.
3. Set the page margins: Top – 1.5cm; Left and Right - 2.5cm; and Bottom - 2.0cm; to optimise space and prevent the CV looking like a narrow column or squeezed between narrow margins.
4. Choose a readable san-serif font – ones without the curly bits – for the whole document. My preference is still Arial; it's easy to read both on-screen and on paper.
5. Select and maintain a single font size throughout with the only variants being bold/not bold; upper and/or lower case. **Nothing less than Arial 11pt.** And don't use italics, boxes or shading!
6. Your name should be in the largest font and bold so, if you prefer to see your name all in capitals, choose a 16pt; or if you prefer to see your name in both upper and lower case, choose an 18pt!
7. It will help to make your contact details easily readable, if you use bold for your name, no bold for your address, bold for your telephone numbers, and no bold for e-mail and LinkedIn.
8. Using a simple line above and below the two paragraphs that summarise you, will subtlety draw the reader's eye to what you have written – true, even for those who say they don't read them!

9. Use the best and most relevant qualifications you have – three lines is probably enough – and there is no need to include any that preceded the main ones – let the space dictate.
10. Please note: One trick, for those without relevant qualifications, is to insert a Career Summary in that position, with the last three positions: Job Title, Company and years from and to.
11. Lift the most appropriate Achievements from earlier sections of this book to populate the rest of page 1.

PRESENTING JOB RELATED INFORMATION

YOUR JOB TITLE, Company Name   **2008 – 2018**

- Your CV should all be about YOU, so your job title is more important than the company name which doesn't need to be in bold.
- Only show the year you started and the year you left – the month of change is not important and gaps in the months distract from what you need them to read.
- Bear in mind that the reader may not know anything about your former employers, so include a two or three-line maximum statement to help them appreciate where you worked.
- The first bullet point under each job, needs to position you within the organisational hierarchy and give an overview of your role, so show it as follows:
- Reported direct to the [Job Title] and responsible for ....
- The word responsible should, ideally, only be used in that one bullet point. Everything else should be presented as an achievement.

GOLDEN RULES FOR CV STRUCTURE

1. Don't let anything on page 1 overlap onto page 2, or from page 2 onto page 3.

2. Don't split a job between pages.

3. Let the space dictate how much information you include, for each job – and limit information on the earliest and less relevant roles to suit.

4. Adding a 2pt space after each bullet point will separate them more clearly and enhance the overall visual impact.

9.

LinkedIn

You are probably aware of LinkedIn already. If not, it is the world's largest business-related, person-to-person, database!

As such, it is used extensively within the Recruitment industry – either to find potential candidates for vacancies they are looking to recruit to, or to check out those people who they have already received applications from.

When a recruiter receives a CV, in direct response to an advertisement or even on a speculative basis, and at first glance think you might be a viable candidate, they will check you out on LinkedIn.

It is absolutely vital, therefore, that there is a level of consistency between the two media, so the recruiter finds the same person appearing in both – and can then expect the same person to walk through their door either for a screening discussion, or a formal job interview. Remember that they are busy people and clearly seek to filter out those who are not a good fit for the role they are seeking candidates for.

Much of the text for your profile can be completed by cutting and pasting from your CV, but the biggest difference between the two is the inclusion of a photograph. Whilst there is no requirement in most countries for CV's to have a photograph, LinkedIn is different!

The simple rule for this modern medium is that if there is no photograph, there is no trust. Try it yourself – find the profile of someone you know who does not have a photograph and see what you think – might you be wondering why no photograph, or are they serious users of LinkedIn?

You might even question whether they are the person you thought you knew, so if it causes you any level of doubt in your mind, think how a potential recruiter/employer might respond. You might try to rationalise against this – but don't forget that these people are very busy and won't spend time doing what you might want them to – they are filtering quickly!

Whilst much of the information required, to complete your LinkedIn profile can be cut and pasted directly from your CV, the one part that many people misuse is the Summary at the start.

Remember that whilst recruiters are visually scanning for information, it is your responsibility to ensure that you give them the information about you that you most want them to know – and that is:

- The level and function of the role you aspire to.
- The industry sectors you have experience/interest in.
- Your key value-adding strengths – where you can make a real difference.

The easiest way to get that across in LinkedIn, is to cut and paste the first paragraph from your CV profile (remember that this, if created according to the guidelines given in earlier chapters, already covers the points above) followed by a heading "Key Value-Adding Strengths" and then insert the headings from your CV as bullet points – just the headings mind, not the details that accompany them on the CV!

With job information, always start each new job with the first bullet point under each job on your CV that should already be reading:

"Reported direct to [Job Title] and responsible for [..................]. Then the reader will have an overview of the job you have been doing.

Then include up to a maximum of five of the bullet-pointed paragraphs relating to each job. Choose the best paragraphs – remember that they will only see and know what you tell them!

Remember: LinkedIn is not only for you to use when you are needing to find and other job. It should be used as a 'living' document – because keeping it up to date, after you have secured your new role, will keep you up to date in the eyes of the recruitment industry; and that's when they might come looking for you!

10.

Conclusion

If you have followed the guidelines in these pages, you will have created a dynamic CV that presents you at your best, for the role you aspire to.

It is your Personal Brand document. It is you – truthfully, clearly, proudly and unashamedly demonstrating how you stand out - head and shoulders above other potential candidates for the same roles.

It cannot guarantee the interview every time, but it will make you more attractive to potential employers because they will see your value to them; and at very least, you will know that not inviting you to interview is truly their loss, not yours.

The key thing to remember now is that you will be entering the job market ahead of the opposition – with a dynamic Personal Brand; and with your skills, knowledge and experience compiled and clearly presented, so the reader will know what you need them to know about you.

There is one more magic element that you are perhaps already aware of, as a result of producing your CV in this way – and that's a growing level of self-confidence, self-esteem and self-worth. You cannot look at what you have written about yourself without feeling a true sense of pride!

Your future is yours to drive, yours to live; and yours to succeed in.

It is a great pleasure for me to play a small part in it with you. I wish you every success, and please share your success stories with me.

Bernard Pearce
info@career-inspirations.co.uk

Look out for the other books in the trilogy:

- Successful Job Searching
- Winning The Interview

Bernard also provides personal one-to-one support to Executives and Senior Managers, to make your Career Transition even smoother for you. Contact him to discuss the challenge you face.

info@career-inspirations.co.uk

Acknowledgements

T his book, the first of a trilogy, has been years in the making; and both friends and family must have wondered whether I was really serious about writing it at all.

Having the idea is one thing and the desire to write it is another; and yet the determination to actually get started was, for one reason or another, delayed for years.

The inspiration and encouragement – which felt like my conscience being poked between the ribs – came from my great friend and mentor Peter Thomson, of Peter Thomson International, the UK's most prolific information product creator. It is, therefore, him that I must first thank, for his help, support and guidance – and for the irritating poke in the ribs!

Peter asked me a very important question before I started – he asked WHY I might want to write it, and the answer came through very clearly.

To enable the reader to:

- Have a better than fighting chance in the job market.
- Beat the hidden barriers to getting the right job.
- Break through corporate glass doors and ceilings.
- Become who they are capable of being.

My commitment to helping executives and senior managers achieve beyond their limitations in the work place was first recognised by Margaret Stead - known as the Dream Architect. She operated years ahead of her time, but sadly passed away a few years ago. She nevertheless deserves my thanks and continuing admiration.

Additionally, all the information in this trilogy of books has been created by observing what doesn't work, designing what might – and then testing it to prove it.

It is also driven by the desire to treat clients as human beings, not numbers; and the belief in giving them the unlimited support they deserve.

I must, therefore, also thank the many hundreds of clients who subjected themselves willingly, though unwittingly, and proved the ideas, techniques and methodologies that have given them some amazing results. It has been a huge honour to work with them and make such a positive difference to their lives.

Finally, I have to thank my friends and family for never giving up on me – and always (they said anyway) believing that I would eventually get started! Their love and support continues to be invaluable.

So finally back to Peter Thomson, thank you - to you and your staff – without whom my expertise and experience might never have made it to the printed page!

About The Author

B ernard Pearce has divided his work so far into two key areas.

The first, within Shell UK, where he was fortunate to work across many divisions – Distribution, Commercial Marketing, Retail Sales, Marketing Communications (including the exploitation of motor sport sponsorship) Sales and Operational Management; and then finally working within HR to help manage the support provided to over 1500 people losing their jobs through rationalisation and downsizing projects.

It was this final role that set the focus for working in Career Transition, drawing on the experience from working across a diverse range of disciplines and functions including distribution, manufacturing, sales, R&D, marketing, finance, legal, HR, shipping and procurement.

Bernard now concentrates his efforts on working with Executives and Senior Managers, because the difference he makes with them should percolate through other layers of the organisation too – and so make a huge difference to many more thousands of people.

His unique and proven expertise has been honed through seeing what doesn't work, developing and proving what might, and then further refining what does.

Whilst recognising that he doesn't have all the answers, Bernard's constant search for new approaches ensures that, if he doesn't have a solution right now, he soon will.

Look out for the other books in the trilogy:

• Successful Job Searching
• Winning The Interview

Bernard also provides personal one-to-one support to Executives and Senior Managers, to make your Career Transition even smoother for you. Contact him to discuss the challenge you face.

info@career-inspirations.co.uk

www.ingramcontent.com/pod-product-compliance
Lightning Source LLC
Chambersburg PA
CBHW071457210326
41597CB00018B/2588